The Artist

Written by Joseph Coelho

Illustrated by Cesar Samaniego

Carl is an artist.

He loves to paint and draw with a **swish** of his brush and a **scribble** of his pencil.

His technique is perfect.

A postcard from his son's family comes sailing through Carl's letterbox,

from deep in the Amazon jungle.

Carl feels his fingers **twitch** with the need to paint ...

feels his mind **popping** with ideas for artistic scenes ...

feels his mouth **smiling** ...

Carl makes bold brushstrokes across his canvas in vivid green. He feels the air around him heat up.

As he splurges the sky with forget-me-not blue, he can feel the humidity rising.

And, before he knows it ...

Carl is in the **deepest,**
greenest, wettest jungle.

And he's being
chased by a jaguar –
inside his painting!

Carl **slides** down the smooth brushstrokes of tree trunks ...

gets **tangled** in a web of watercolour vines ...

sings with the multicoloured birds in the trees ...

5

... and emerges safely back home.

The following day, Carl receives a postcard from his daughter and her family, on holiday amongst the mountains and rivers of Norway.

Carl feels his fingers **twitch** ...

feels his mind **popping** ...

feels his mouth **smiling** ...

Carl starts to paint.

Using an impressionist style of short, quick dabs, he dots the river water in aquamarine, snaking through the foreground of the landscape. He feels the air get icy.

As he uses long, rough brushstrokes in flint grey to create mountains that loom in the background, he feels snow tingle on the back of his neck.

And, before he knows it ...

Carl is **swooshing** down a mountainside!

He's doing **flips** and **somersaults** over ivory acrylic-paint snow dunes,

swerving past ink-black mountains.

Carl **zig-zags** through a forest of seaweed-green pine ...

skids over ice of the deepest azure blue ...

races towards a cliff edge ...

Will he tumble over the side?

He **slides** just in time ... out of the painting ...

... and safely
back home.

The following day,
Carl receives a postcard
from his brother,

who is trekking through
the Sahara desert.

Carl feels his fingers **twitch** with the need to try new methods ...

feels his mind **popping** with ideas for new subjects ...

feels his mouth **smiling**.

Carl stipples the canvas with orange.
He feels the air around him heat up again.

As he paints huge
hills of sand in the
middle ground, he feels
a warm, dry breeze.

And, before he knows it ...

Carl is **racing** over the dunes in a sand buggy, past the slithering fine brushstrokes of snakes and roughly sketched scorpions.

He's **zooming** to an oasis
     in the middle of the desert

       where palm trees sway,
         with their finger-painted dates.

Carl is **hurtling** towards a pool of white-highlighted water ...

... but it's just a mirage!
It's not real.

Carl **tumbles** out of the painting, smiling and laughing ...

... and is met by some familiar faces!

His son and his family are back from the Amazon,
suntanned and smiling.

His daughter and her family are back from Norway,
with photos from their adventures.

His brother is grinning,
and pouring the sand from his boots!

Carl shows them all his paintings, inspired by their postcards.
They gaze at the thick splurges of paint and the finely drawn details.

Carl has had an amazing time on his artistic adventures.

It's like he was with them all along ...

and now they share,

with artistic flair,

their stories.

But what's this
coming through
the letterbox?

It's a postcard of a seascape from
Carl's cousin, who is in Australia ...
diving with sharks!

15

Published by Pearson Education Limited, 80 Strand, London, WC2R 0RL.

www.pearsonschools.co.uk

Text © Pearson Education Limited 2020

Written by Joseph Coelho

Project managed and edited by Just Content Limited

Original illustrations © Pearson Education Limited 2020

Illustrated by Cesar Samaniego

Designed and typeset by Collaborate Agency Limited

First published 2020

23 22 21 20

10 9 8 7 6 5 4 3 2 1

British Library Cataloguing in Publication Data

A catalogue record for this book is available from the British Library

ISBN 978 0 435 20151 7

Printed in Slovakia by Neografia

Note from the publisher

Pearson has robust editorial processes, including answer and fact checks, to ensure the accuracy of the content in this publication, and every effort is made to ensure this publication is free of errors. We are, however, only human, and occasionally errors do occur. Pearson is not liable for any misunderstandings that arise as a result of errors in this publication, but it is our priority to ensure that the content is accurate. If you spot an error, please do contact us at resourcescorrections@pearson.com so we can make sure it is corrected.